MW00889188

Be

Encouraged

Beloved

Sam C. Robinson

—

SCAC Publishing

Be Encouraged Beloved

DEDICATION

To my beloved parents, Jay and Ines, you were gone too soon from my life but remain an eternal encouragement to my heart. I remember you well.

Be Encouraged Beloved

Table of Contents

Introduction

Be Encouraged Beloved

There are times in life when we are overwhelmed. Life does not always present experiences that are easy to manage and/or maneuver. There are many people who need encouragement but lack being encouraged. Sometimes, the end result is low morale. It is natural to expect the support and encouragement from the people you know and love. However, there will be moments when we must encourage ourselves.

In 1 Samuel 30, David encountered a time when he had to encourage himself. Just like David, when we have experienced loss after following the will of God, encouragement can become hard to come by amongst friends and family, especially if they too are affected by personal loss.

Be Encouraged Beloved

This daily journal encompasses a section of focus such as: Love, Friends, Adversity, and more. Each day, as you read the daily inspiration of the day; meditate for fifteen minutes, reflect and write your thoughts. It is proven that writing is an affirmative way to scribe things upon the tablet of your heart. Through your reflection and writings, you too will find these words encouraging and enlightening that you are God's beloved.

Be Encouraged Beloved

Love

Psalm 136

Thanksgiving to God for His Enduring Mercy

Oh, give thanks to the LORD, for *He is* good!
For His mercy *endures* forever.
[2] Oh, give thanks to the God of gods!
For His mercy *endures* forever.
[3] Oh, give thanks to the Lord of lords!
For His mercy *endures* forever:

[4] To Him who alone does great wonders,
For His mercy *endures* forever;
[5] To Him who by wisdom made the heavens,
For His mercy *endures* forever;
[6] To Him who laid out the earth above the waters,
For His mercy *endures* forever;
[7] To Him who made great lights,
For His mercy *endures* forever—
[8] The sun to rule by day,
For His mercy *endures* forever;
[9] The moon and stars to rule by night,
For His mercy *endures* forever.

[10] To Him who struck Egypt in their firstborn,
For His mercy *endures* forever;
[11] And brought out Israel from among them,
For His mercy *endures* forever;
[12] With a strong hand, and with an outstretched arm,
For His mercy *endures* forever;

Be Encouraged Beloved

[13] To Him who divided the Red Sea in two,
For His mercy *endures* forever;
[14] And made Israel pass through the midst of it,
For His mercy *endures* forever;
[15] But overthrew Pharaoh and his army in the Red Sea,
For His mercy *endures* forever;
[16] To Him who led His people through the wilderness,
For His mercy *endures* forever;
[17] To Him who struck down great kings,
For His mercy *endures* forever;
[18] And slew famous kings,
For His mercy *endures* forever—
[19] Sihon king of the Amorites,
For His mercy *endures* forever;
[20] And Og king of Bashan,
For His mercy *endures* forever—
[21] And gave their land as a heritage,
For His mercy *endures* forever;
[22] A heritage to Israel His servant,
For His mercy *endures* forever.

[23] Who remembered us in our lowly state,
For His mercy *endures* forever;
[24] And rescued us from our enemies,
For His mercy *endures* forever;
[25] Who gives food to all flesh,
For His mercy *endures* forever.

[26] Oh, give thanks to the God of heaven!
For His mercy *endures* forever.

Be Encouraged Beloved

Day 1 Reflection

Be *Encouraged* Beloved,

Many days you may feel like you are alone in this world but Jesus promises never to leave you or forsake you.

He also sends special people to stand with you during the hardest times. Apostle Paul said when all men forsook him, the Lord stood with Him.

Never underestimate the value of having God stand with you. He is more than the whole world against you.

In my best preaching squall, NOT TODAY DEVIL! GOD IS WITH ME!!!

*Reflect on one time of being alone, then write about how you overcame loneliness. Or write 5 declarations to override loneliness.

_____

_____

_____

_____

Be Encouraged Beloved

Be Encouraged Beloved

Day 2 Reflection

Be *Encouraged* Beloved,

Within each of our communities, we have experienced great hurt and loss due to death of loved ones. Even if we are not directly affected, by reading our local obituaries, we can know that someone is affected every day. Pray for one another to be comforted and pray to be a comfort.

Yes, it's true that it is appointed to man to die once but we must remember the opportunity of life that we receive every day with God's new mercy. We must also remember that the judgment comes after death. Living a life that is pleasing to God is possible with faith in God. He has purpose for each of us...with expectations filled with goodness and not evil.

*Write about what it means to you to live a life pleasing unto God.

_____

_____

_____

Be Encouraged Beloved

Day 3 Reflection

Be *Encouraged* Beloved,

We are not in "this" by ourselves. Even though many people "walk" away, turn backs, and abandon us at times. Yes, it even hurts when friends, family, and foes reveal betrayal from within.

However, I am so glad to witness that the Lord never leaves us nor forsakes us. He is always there to help, encourage, assist, cover, protect, nurture, and love us. The Lord is consistent, not wavering, and steady to be an immediate presence in our time of trouble. Amazingly enough, He is there even when there is no trouble. Oh bless His name!

Steady yourself in trusting the Lord to be faithful. He won't let you down! I will trust in the Lord, until I die (and live again)! He has proven himself to be trustworthy for us all.

*Write about the benefit of trusting in the Lord.

Be Encouraged Beloved

Be Encouraged Beloved

Day 4 Reflection

Be *Encouraged* Beloved,

Jesus came to mend the brokenhearted. Yours won't
be broken forever. Give Him time to work!

*What was it like when your heart was broken? What happened
to break your heart and how did you heal?

_____

_____

_____

_____

_____

_____

_____

_____

_____

_____

_____

_____

Be Encouraged Beloved

Be Encouraged Beloved

Friendship

Be Encouraged Beloved

Psalm

**To the Chief Musician. With stringed instruments. A
Contemplation of David.**

Give ear to my prayer, O God,
And do not hide Yourself from my supplication.
[2] Attend to me, and hear me;
I am restless in my complaint, and moan noisily,
[3] Because of the voice of the enemy,
Because of the oppression of the wicked;
For they bring down trouble upon me,
And in wrath they hate me.

[4] My heart is severely pained within me,
And the terrors of death have fallen upon me.
[5] Fearfulness and trembling have come upon me,
And horror has overwhelmed me.
[6] So I said, "Oh, that I had wings like a dove!
I would fly away and be at rest.
[7] Indeed, I would wander far off,
And remain in the wilderness. *Selah*
[8] I would hasten my escape
From the windy storm *and* tempest."

[9] Destroy, O Lord, *and* divide their tongues,
For I have seen violence and strife in the city.
[10] Day and night they go around it on its walls;
Iniquity and trouble *are* also in the midst of it.
[11] Destruction *is* in its midst;
Oppression and deceit do not depart from its streets.

[12] For *it is* not an enemy *who* reproaches me;
Then I could bear *it.*
Nor *is it* one *who* hates me who has exalted *himself* against
me;

Be Encouraged Beloved

Then I could hide from him.
[13] But *it was* you, a man my equal,
My companion and my acquaintance.
[14] We took sweet counsel together,
And walked to the house of God in the throng.

[15] Let death seize them;
Let them go down alive into hell,
For wickedness *is* in their dwellings *and* among them.

[16] As for me, I will call upon God,
And the LORD shall save me.
[17] Evening and morning and at noon
I will pray, and cry aloud,
And He shall hear my voice.
[18] He has redeemed my soul in peace from the battle *that
was* against me,
For there were many against me.
[19] God will hear, and afflict them,
Even He who abides from of old. *Selah*
Because they do not change,
Therefore they do not fear God.

[20] He has put forth his hands against those who were at
peace with him;
He has broken his covenant.
[21] *The words* of his mouth were smoother than butter,
But war *was* in his heart;
His words were softer than oil,
Yet they *were* drawn swords.

[22] Cast your burden on the LORD,
And He shall sustain you;
He shall never permit the righteous to be moved.

Be Encouraged Beloved

[23] But You, O God, shall bring them down to the pit of destruction;
Bloodthirsty and deceitful men shall not live out half their days;
But I will trust in You.

Be Encouraged Beloved

Day 5 Reflection

Be *Encouraged* Beloved,

Even when the ones that say they love you the most hurt you, God still has a plan for you. "They smile in your face and all the time"...well you know the rest.

However, He is our shield and buckler! Shake those snakes off into the fire like Apostle Paul.

*Write about the ways that God has protected you.

Be Encouraged Beloved

Day 6 Reflection

Be *Encouraged* Beloved,

Sometimes the shock from how others treat you can knock the wind out of you and cause you to tremble inside but do not fear; you are stronger than their actions.

Be strong in the Lord and the power of His might. In as much as they have done it to the least of these, they have done it unto God.

*Everyone needs encouragement sometimes, write 12 things that would encourage someone in hard times.

_____

_____

_____

_____

_____

_____

_____

_____

_____

Be Encouraged Beloved

Be Encouraged Beloved

Day 7 Reflection

Be *Encouraged* Beloved,

Friendship with God is better than friendship with mankind. Often misunderstood yet having to stand regardless builds immeasurable strength within you.

Be strong in the Lord and the power of his might. In as much as they have done it to the least of these, they have done it unto God.

*Being strong in the Lord will take you through hard times. Describe a moment when you stood strong in the Lord.

_____ .

_____

_____

_____

_____

_____

_____

_____

Be Encouraged Beloved

Be Encouraged Beloved

Day 8 Reflection

Be *Encouraged* Beloved,

Sometimes the shock of how others treat you can knock the wind out of you and cause you to tremble inside but do not fear; you are stronger than their actions.

*How do you recover from rejection?

_____

_____

_____

_____

_____

_____

_____

_____

_____

_____

Be Encouraged Beloved

Be Encouraged Beloved

Hope

Psalm 25

A Plea for Deliverance and Forgiveness

A Psalm of David.

To You, O LORD, I lift up my soul.
² O my God, I trust in You;
Let me not be ashamed;
Let not my enemies triumph over me.
³ Indeed, let no one who waits on You be ashamed;
Let those be ashamed who deal treacherously without cause.

⁴ Show me Your ways, O LORD;
Teach me Your paths.
⁵ Lead me in Your truth and teach me,
For You *are* the God of my salvation;
On You I wait all the day.

⁶ Remember, O LORD, Your tender mercies and Your loving kindnesses,
For they *are* from of old.
⁷ Do not remember the sins of my youth, nor my transgressions;
According to Your mercy remember me,
For Your goodness' sake, O LORD.

⁸ Good and upright *is* the LORD;
Therefore He teaches sinners in the way.
⁹ The humble He guides in justice,
And the humble He teaches His way.
¹⁰ All the paths of the LORD *are* mercy and truth,
To such as keep His covenant and His testimonies.

Be Encouraged Beloved

[11] For Your name's sake, O LORD,
Pardon my iniquity, for it *is* great.

[12] Who *is* the man that fears the LORD?
Him shall He teach in the way He chooses.
[13] He himself shall dwell in prosperity,
And his descendants shall inherit the earth.
[14] The secret of the LORD *is* with those who fear Him,
And He will show them His covenant.
[15] My eyes *are* ever toward the LORD,
For He shall pluck my feet out of the net.

[16] Turn Yourself to me, and have mercy on me,
For I *am* desolate and afflicted.
[17] The troubles of my heart have enlarged;
Bring me out of my distresses!
[18] Look on my affliction and my pain,
And forgive all my sins.
[19] Consider my enemies, for they are many;
And they hate me with cruel hatred.
[20] Keep my soul, and deliver me;
Let me not be ashamed, for I put my trust in You.
[21] Let integrity and uprightness preserve me,
For I wait for You.

[22] Redeem Israel, O God,
Out of all their troubles!

Be Encouraged Beloved

Day 9 Reflection

Be *Encouraged* Beloved,

There is no panic in heaven. God does not have problems but He does have a plan.

*How do you define resting in the Lord?

_____

_____

_____

_____

_____

_____

_____

_____

_____

_____

_____

_____

_____

Be Encouraged Beloved

Be Encouraged Beloved

Day 10 Reflection

Be *Encouraged* Beloved,

Brothers are born for adversity! If you can't run with me in my "trouble" then definitely believe you will not stand with me in my "triumph".

*How did you feel when you had to separate from a friendship or relationship that you enjoyed?

_____

_____

_____

_____

_____

_____

_____

_____

_____

_____

_____

Be Encouraged Beloved

Day 11 Reflection

Be *Encouraged* Beloved,

You lived through it, it wasn't strong enough to kill you or else it would have destroyed you. God's hand over your life is stronger than what rises against you.

*Recant the time when you know that God defeated your enemy.

_____

_____

_____

_____

_____

_____

_____

_____

_____

_____

_____

_____

Be Encouraged Beloved

Be Encouraged Beloved

Day 12 Reflection

Be *Encouraged* Beloved,

It's the MOST wonderful time of the year!!!
The truth of the matter is that anytime can be the
most wonderful time...

The MOST wonderful time to share the hope of
Christ...
The MOST wonderful time to share the love of Christ
and good tidings to our fellow man...

The MOST wonderful time to remember that God
sent His son for us with purpose to deliver us...

Many still do not know Christ...take this as your
MOST wonderful time to share Jesus with someone
else.

*How does Christ minister to you or others in the world today?

_____

_____

Be Encouraged Beloved

Be Encouraged Beloved

Hurt

Psalm 5

A Prayer for Guidance

To the Chief Musician. With flutes. A Psalm of David.

Give ear to my words, O LORD,
Consider my meditation.
[2] Give heed to the voice of my cry,
My King and my God,
For to You I will pray.
[3] My voice You shall hear in the morning, O LORD;
In the morning I will direct *it* to You,
And I will look up.

[4] For You *are* not a God who takes pleasure in wickedness,
Nor shall evil dwell with You.
[5] The boastful shall not stand in Your sight;
You hate all workers of iniquity.
[6] You shall destroy those who speak falsehood;
The LORD abhors the bloodthirsty and deceitful man.

[7] But as for me, I will come into Your house in the
multitude of Your mercy;
In fear of You I will worship toward Your holy temple.
[8] Lead me, O LORD, in Your righteousness because of my
enemies;
Make Your way straight before my face.

[9] For *there is* no faithfulness in their mouth;
Their inward part *is* destruction;
Their throat *is* an open tomb;
They flatter with their tongue.
[10] Pronounce them guilty, O God!
Let them fall by their own counsels;

Be Encouraged Beloved

Cast them out in the multitude of their transgressions,
For they have rebelled against You.

[11] But let all those rejoice who put their trust in You;
Let them ever shout for joy, because You defend them;
Let those also who love Your name
Be joyful in You.
[12] For You, O LORD, will bless the righteous;
With favor You will surround him as *with* a shield.

Be Encouraged Beloved

Day 13 Reflection

Be *Encouraged* Beloved,

Sometimes people may not care much about what you are going through but do not worry over that matter. One who has unreliable friends will soon come to a ruin but there is a friend that sticks closer than a brother. Depend on the friend that is truly reliable.

You can cast your cares on him for HE CARES FOR YOU! Have a little talk with Jesus and tell Him all about your troubles. He hears and he answers!

*Write your own prayer. In the prayer, apply 3 scriptures about God's promise.

_____

_____

_____

_____

_____

_____

Be Encouraged Beloved

Be Encouraged Beloved

Day 14 Reflection

Be *Encouraged* Beloved,

All things work together for the good of them who love the Lord and are called according to His purpose. As long as you meet those criteria, everything will work for you and not against you. Let it become a part of your testimony!

*What is the greatest victory that you've experienced? Give details of the dilemma and the victory.

_____

_____

_____

_____

_____

_____

_____

_____

_____

Be Encouraged Beloved

Day 15 Reflection

Be *Encouraged* Beloved,

While others may treat you as if you do not matter and make a difference; God had and has you in His mind and heart because you matter to Him.

Who is more important? Him or them?

*In this reflection, write about a time when you made God more important than your trial.

_____

_____

_____

_____

_____

_____

_____

_____

_____

_____

_____

Be Encouraged Beloved

Be Encouraged Beloved

Day 16 Reflection

Be *Encouraged* Beloved,

When God is doing something authentic in your life, the devil will always attempt to send a counterfeit to distract you. Just be faithful and trust the Spirit of God to lead you in His perfect will.

Proverbs 3:5-6
Trust in the LORD with all your heart, and do not lean on your own understanding. In all your ways acknowledge him, and he will make straight your paths. He will direct you through every area necessary to accomplish His will and purpose.

*Do you think it is hard to trust in the Lord? Or what are some principles a person can apply to help them better trust the Lord?

_____

_____

_____

_____

_____

Be Encouraged Beloved

Enemies

Psalm 59

The Assured Judgment of the Wicked

To the Chief Musician. Set to "Do Not Destroy." A Michtam of David when Saul sent men, and they watched the house in order to kill him.

Deliver me from my enemies, O my God; Defend me from those who rise up against me.
[2] Deliver me from the workers of iniquity,
And save me from bloodthirsty men.

[3] For look, they lie in wait for my life;
The mighty gather against me,
Not *for* my transgression nor *for* my sin, O LORD.
[4] They run and prepare themselves through no fault *of mine.*

Awake to help me, and behold!
[5] You therefore, O LORD God of hosts, the God of Israel,
Awake to punish all the nations;
Do not be merciful to any wicked transgressors. *Selah*

[6] At evening they return,
They growl like a dog,
And go all around the city.
[7] Indeed, they belch with their mouth;
Swords *are* in their lips;
For *they say,* "Who hears?"

[8] But You, O LORD, shall laugh at them;
You shall have all the nations in derision.
[9] I will wait for You, O You his Strength;
For God *is* my defense.

Be Encouraged Beloved

[10] My God of mercy shall come to meet me;
God shall let me see *my desire* on my enemies.

[11] Do not slay them, lest my people forget;
Scatter them by Your power,
And bring them down,
O Lord our shield.
[12] *For* the sin of their mouth *and* the words of their lips,
Let them even be taken in their pride,
And for the cursing and lying *which* they speak.
[13] Consume *them* in wrath, consume *them,*
That they *may* not *be;*
And let them know that God rules in Jacob
To the ends of the earth. *Selah*

[14] And at evening they return,
They growl like a dog,
And go all around the city.
[15] They wander up and down for food,
And howl if they are not satisfied.

[16] But I will sing of Your power;
Yes, I will sing aloud of Your mercy in the morning;
For You have been my defense
And refuge in the day of my trouble.
[17] To You, O my Strength, I will sing praises;
For God *is* my defense,
My God of mercy.

Day 17 Reflection

Be *Encouraged* Beloved,

Our future looks brighter than our past. Let the past be a great resource for growth and productivity. We learn from our past, we grow from our past, and we move beyond our past to grasp great futures.

We can't afford to allow our past experiences to cripple us from living life in "forward" motion. It is the past and that part is done and over. It isn't a place for us to stay and dwell.

It is possible to get beyond the past. If looking back keeps you from moving forward, don't look back until you can handle it without going back.

*What hinders you from looking forward and moving forward?

_____

_____

_____

Be Encouraged Beloved

Be Encouraged Beloved

Day 18 Reflection

Be *Encouraged* Beloved,

God is not through with US yet!!! So many times, we make mistakes and then the enemy (through circumstances and/or others) tries to convince us that we have come to the "end".

On the contrary, it is NOT the "end" but it is perfect time to BEGIN AGAIN. It is a grand time to ask God to "start us over".

SO...get up, wipe your tears, breathe again, dust off, get rid of that which hindered us in the first place, and take a step FORWARD in FAITH. It is better to walk away from it than to wallow in it.

Beloved, I know you (we) can do it! God is with us because He loves us most and best of all.

*Write you greatest memory of a demonstration of God's love.

_____

_____

Be Encouraged Beloved

Be Encouraged Beloved

Day 19 Reflection

Be *Encouraged* Beloved,

Just like Joseph who had brothers that hated him for his favor, you will have brethren who hate you for yours. However, when it really mattered, it was not Joseph's favor that saved their lives; it was his ability to have mercy.

God's favor saved Joseph's life and mercy saved the life of his brothers. There will always come a point when we ALL need mercy.

Remember, what others mean for evil, God means for good to save the lives of many. Blessed are the merciful for they shall obtain mercy.

*What was it like when you had to apply mercy in a situation that angered or frustrated you?

_____

_____

_____

Be Encouraged Beloved

Be Encouraged Beloved

Day 20 Reflection

Be *Encouraged* Beloved,

Pain has a great way of reminding us that we have purpose. Keep focused. Use it! Let the pain help produce purpose.

*Write about five ways to overcome emotional pain.

_____

_____

_____

_____

_____

_____

_____

_____

_____

_____

_____

_____

_____

Be Encouraged Beloved

Be Encouraged Beloved

God

Be Encouraged Beloved

Psalm 99

Praise to the LORD for His Holiness

The LORD reigns;
Let the peoples tremble!
He dwells *between* the cherubim;
Let the earth be moved!
[2] The LORD *is* great in Zion,
And He *is* high above all the peoples.
[3] Let them praise Your great and awesome name—
He *is* holy.

[4] The King's strength also loves justice;
You have established equity;
You have executed justice and righteousness in Jacob.
[5] Exalt the LORD our God,
And worship at His footstool—
He *is* holy.

[6] Moses and Aaron were among His priests,
And Samuel was among those who called upon His name;
They called upon the LORD, and He answered them.
[7] He spoke to them in the cloudy pillar;
They kept His testimonies and the ordinance He gave them.

[8] You answered them, O LORD our God;
You were to them God-Who-Forgives,
Though You took vengeance on their deeds.
[9] Exalt the LORD our God,
And worship at His holy hill;
For the LORD our God *is* holy

Be Encouraged Beloved

Day 21 Reflection

Be *Encouraged* Beloved,

As you remain steadfast to share the truth of the Lord with others, always know there will be some that will not receive for whatever reason.

Yes, in these times, there will be many who will not endure sound doctrine. Reach those you can because they are receptive and pray for those who reject truth. We know it is better to be a fool than an unteachable person who is wise in their own eyes.

Let your encouragement rest in seeing lives transformed by the renewing of their minds. That is the goal of the Kingdom. I am a witness!

*What two times when encouragement changed your mind or your outlook on life or a situation?

_____

_____

_____

_____

Be Encouraged Beloved

Be Encouraged Beloved

Day 22 Reflection

Be *Encouraged* Beloved,

When you feel overwhelmed and bombarded by life's circumstances, remember there is a higher place than yourself to go to and remain steady. Stand on the solid rock that never breaks down. (Psalm 62:1)

*What is the last bible scripture that you've read? Write what that scripture means to you. How did you stand on that "solid rock"?

_____

_____

_____

_____

_____

_____

_____

_____

_____

Be Encouraged Beloved

Day 23 Reflection

Be *Encouraged* Beloved,

Living up to the expectations of mankind won't do you any good if our Lord, Jesus, will not be able to say well done thy good and faithful servant. His expectations matter more.

*How does the thought of hearing those glorious words, "Well Done" make you feel?

Be Encouraged Beloved

Be Encouraged Beloved

Day 24 Reflection

Be *Encouraged* Beloved,

When people set you up to hurt you, God uses it to help you! They may plan the trap but it will be for God's use to give you a triumphant victory. Do not fret. All things work together...

*Do you recall a time when God turn the odds in your favor?

_____

_____

_____

_____

_____

_____

_____

_____

_____

_____

_____

Be Encouraged Beloved

Adversity

Psalm 31

The LORD a Fortress in Adversity

To the Chief Musician. A Psalm of David.

In You, O LORD, I put my trust;
Let me never be ashamed;
Deliver me in Your righteousness.
² Bow down Your ear to me,
Deliver me speedily;
Be my rock of refuge,
A fortress of defense to save me.

³ For You *are* my rock and my fortress;
Therefore, for Your name's sake,
Lead me and guide me.
⁴ Pull me out of the net which they have secretly laid for me,
For You *are* my strength.
⁵ Into Your hand I commit my spirit;
You have redeemed me, O LORD God of truth.

⁶ I have hated those who regard useless idols;
But I trust in the LORD.
⁷ I will be glad and rejoice in Your mercy,
For You have considered my trouble;
You have known my soul in adversities,
⁸ And have not shut me up into the hand of the enemy;
You have set my feet in a wide place.

⁹ Have mercy on me, O LORD, for I am in trouble;
My eye wastes away with grief,
Yes, my soul and my body!
¹⁰ For my life is spent with grief,

Be Encouraged Beloved

And my years with sighing;
My strength fails because of my iniquity,
And my bones waste away.
[11] I am a reproach among all my enemies,
But especially among my neighbors,
And *am* repulsive to my acquaintances;
Those who see me outside flee from me.
[12] I am forgotten like a dead man, out of mind;
I am like a broken vessel.
[13] For I hear the slander of many;
Fear *is* on every side;
While they take counsel together against me,
They scheme to take away my life.

[14] But as for me, I trust in You, O LORD;
I say, "You *are* my God."
[15] My times *are* in Your hand;
Deliver me from the hand of my enemies,
And from those who persecute me.
[16] Make Your face shine upon Your servant;
Save me for Your mercies' sake.
[17] Do not let me be ashamed, O LORD, for I have called
upon You;
Let the wicked be ashamed;
Let them be silent in the grave.
[18] Let the lying lips be put to silence,
Which speak insolent things proudly and contemptuously
against the righteous.

[19] Oh, how great *is* Your goodness,
Which You have laid up for those who fear You,
Which You have prepared for those who trust in You
In the presence of the sons of men!
[20] You shall hide them in the secret place of Your presence
From the plots of man;

Be Encouraged Beloved

You shall keep them secretly in a pavilion
From the strife of tongues.

[21] Blessed *be* the LORD,
For He has shown me His marvelous kindness in a strong
city!
[22] For I said in my haste,
"I am cut off from before Your eyes";
Nevertheless You heard the voice of my supplications
When I cried out to You.

[23] Oh, love the LORD, all you His saints!
For the LORD preserves the faithful,
And fully repays the proud person.
[24] Be of good courage,
And He shall strengthen your heart,
All you who hope in the LORD

Be Encouraged Beloved

Day 25 Reflection

Be *Encouraged* Beloved,

Some moments in life will leave you speechless but the good thing is that those are also the moments where there is no need for words. Study to be quiet, remain humble under the mighty hand of God, and receive the peace that God brings to your mind, heart, and soul.

*Why do you think it is hard for us to be silent in times when we need to be silent?

_____

_____

_____

_____

_____

_____

_____

_____

_____

Be Encouraged Beloved

Be Encouraged Beloved

Day 26 Reflection

Be *Encouraged* Beloved,

God knows your end from the beginning. Never let another determine your end by what they know nothing about! God knows and He determines your end!

*List 5 characteristics of the end times according to the bible.

_____

_____

_____

_____

_____

_____

_____

_____

_____

_____

_____

_____

Be Encouraged Beloved

Be Encouraged Beloved

Be *Encouraged* Beloved,

What happened to you may have been unfortunate, unforeseen, and even unheard of, BUT it will not undo God's will for your life.

*How do you define God's Perfect Will? What is God's will for your life?

_____

_____

_____

_____

_____

_____

_____

_____

_____

_____

_____

_____

_____

Be Encouraged Beloved

_____

_____

_____

_____

_____

_____

_____

_____

_____

_____

_____

_____

_____

_____

_____

_____

_____

_____

Day 28 Reflection

Be *Encouraged* Beloved,

There will be challenges in this journey, but we still come out with victory. Take a deep breath, dig deeper, pray more, and believe...

Come on through!

*What were your three greatest challenges? How did you win?

_____

_____

_____

_____

_____

_____

_____

_____

_____

_____

_____

_____

Be Encouraged Beloved

Be Encouraged Beloved

Day 29 Reflection

Be *Encouraged* Beloved,

Destiny overrides disaster! The destiny God has for you is permanent and eternal. At the time of life's damaging disasters, He still knows how to deliver and walk you through.

There may be "debris and dirt" but rest assured, the detour will also get you to your final destination. All of this has a purpose in your destiny.

*What are three thing that you would like to accomplish in the next two years?

_____

_____

_____

_____

_____

_____

_____

_____

Be Encouraged Beloved

Be Encouraged Beloved

Day 30 Reflection

Be *Encouraged* Beloved,

His word still stands! It lasts forever! Heaven and earth will pass away before one jot or tittle of His word fails. He watches over His word to perform it!

Now, focus...Remember what He said about you!

*Give one example or situation of His word never failing in your life?

_____

_____

_____

_____

_____

_____

_____

Be Encouraged Beloved

Conclusion

Be Encouraged Beloved

Ecclesiastes mentions that life is but a vapor. Once we have experienced life's up's and down's, there is no need to sit around discouraged. There are many who wished they had an opportunity to live. As long as you can breathe, you have enough strength and opportunity to encourage yourself.

Rather than complaining, spend your energy deciding how you are going to possess and occupy your destiny. There is an exact blessing in being God's beloved. He does not abandon you or leave you comfortless. Spending too much time counting on others can cause you to discount yourself.

Endurance can be built by encouragement received. Enduring through the hardest challenges and the most difficult situations can better be made possible by the

Be Encouraged Beloved

slightest bit of encouragement. You are encouraged to keep moving forward and setting the goal to make it to the end of your experience knowing you have been beloved all the way through.

Beloved, remember, giving yourself fifteen minutes of uninterrupted time can produce the outcome that you desire. Remaining encouraged is not the responsibility of your family or friends. However, it should become a duty and privilege to mandate for yourself; to remain encouraged and strengthened until He returns!

Be Encouraged Beloved

About the Author &

Booking

About the Author

Pastor Samantha Robinson is a true testament of survival.

Having been orphaned at a young age, she has continued to build family relationships throughout the Kingdom. She commands dead things to live. Pastor Robinson is not just a mere role model but she is the model. Her personal motto: "God does give second chances more than once!"

Her academic accomplishments cause her to push young people to becoming all that they can be and encourage those who are mature in age to never quit. She is the recipient of a Bachelor's degree in Business Administration from NC Wesleyan College, Bachelor's degree in Biblical Studies from Bethel Bible College, as well as a Masters of Divinity degree from Shaw University Divinity School. She is currently pursuing her Doctorate in Christian Education from Liberty University.

Her skillset cannot be overshadowed by the anointing set upon her life. She is a sought-out conference speaker, financial management professional, ministry training and development coordinator, and efficient in workshop presentation.

Pastor Samantha Robinson who is more affectionately known as "Pastor Sam" to many, doesn't pride herself on her achievements. Instead, she strives to preach the gospel to save the lost, set the captives free, and heal the hurting. As she administers the Word, God unctions the prophetic call upon her life to decree and establish the mandates of God. She is not just any woman but she is undoubtedly "God's Woman." She has yielded her life to be used by God as His catalyst for His glory and a dominating voice over the enemy that comes to steal, kill and destroy God's

children.

Booking Information

To book Sam C. Robinson, MDiv., for your next event, email **2booksamc@gmail.com**.

73106261R00054

Made in the USA
Columbia, SC
08 September 2019